NO MORE WAR GAMES

by Mario Murillo

ANTHONY DOUGLAS PUBLISHERS
c/o P.O. Box 5027, San Ramon, CA 94583

NO MORE WAR GAMES
Copyright © 1987 by Mario Murillo

Published by Anthony Douglas Publishers
c/o P.O. Box 5027, San Ramon, CA 94583

Printed in the United States of America

CONTENTS

INTRODUCTION

There is a serious problem in the Christian world today. People have found the real life of faith entirely different from the panacea promised in many seminars or on tape recordings. Charismatic Christians especially are finding the warfare much more intense than they ever expected or were taught about. Few anticipated the recent scandals; not many were prepared for the rash of media attacks on the Holy Spirit movement. Heap on all this the daily grind of modern life and you quickly see the potential for disaster.

Where is the authority we boasted of? Can we find the real faith to replace this hollow believism? What we have is an epidemic of shallowness; we must answer many life and death issues and we must answer them now.

Jesus' disciples went through a similar ordeal. They all but glided through three and a half years of unchallenged success. The Lord ended their kindergarten when He said, "One of you will betray Me." This began the chain of unexpected crises that ended with the crucifixion. Ultimately, the disciples did pass the test and know the real meaning of victory; they did learn to walk in legitimate authority and we can too!

1

Like it or not, the easy era is over. Millions of American believers must face their need for an immovable anchor. Push all the buttons; recite all the formulas you want, as sincerely as you can, but it will not work. Without God's endorsement on our warfare, we might as well pound a glass nail. Only forged character will prevail. Only God-imparted faith will penetrate the enemy. To go from hype to true spiritual power requires brutal personal honesty. The cheap thrill and the instant cure must be abandoned. No one should discard their conviction that triumph is available to us today.

We can become the dread of demons and a delight to our mighty God. This book is a call for a full-hearted pursuit of gold tried in the fire.

". . . but the people who know their God shall be strong and carry out great exploits." (Daniel 11:13 NKJ)

Mario Murillo
November, 1987

NO MORE WAR GAMES

"The Christian life is *like* a war!" People often say that but they have no idea how dangerous that statement is. It is close enough to the truth to seem right but it leaves us vulnerable where it really matters.

Many of us fight a symbolic battle, pray figurative prayers, and ceremonially train for conflict.

The Christian life is not like a war; it, in fact, is a war!

A shock comes when our synthetic warring collides with a "real" Satan who knows this is not a war game.

"Be sober, be vigilant; because your adversary the devil, as a roaring lion, walketh about, seeking whom he may devour." (I Peter 5:8)

After suffering a severe attack, many believers accuse God of failing or going back on His Word. But the failure is not God's; *the fault lies in the fact that we have filtered scripture through our cultural preoccupation with escape.*

The needed information was there for us all the time. The Bible teaches warfare. Triumph is promised but only if we learn to fight a good fight!

"Fight the good fight of faith, lay hold on eternal life, whereunto thou art also called, and hast professed a

3

good profession before many witnesses."
(I Timothy 6:12)

"Escape" is the key word because Americans long to escape. We want to avoid effort, struggle, confrontation; in essence, we want to escape war.

We believe in the instant cure: the right pill, the appropriate button. Whereas character and greatness were once the product of the furnace of affliction, we now seek to microwave them into existence. It is a fantasy to want the benefits of effort without actually exerting effort and to want triumph without contending for it according to the rules.

America is finding out that escapism quickly reduces its victims to addicts without incentive. Life is an equal opportunity destroyer. Everyone will have a turn at a crisis that will reveal the substance of their foundation. Hollow anchors will fail; stage props will fail; and our false cures will explode when we need them most.

Within the last fifty years, escapism has seeped into American pulpits. The real war has become *like* a war. Instantism promises believers undisciplined protection and automatic maturity.

In the past, conversion meant deliverance from eternal doom and slavery to Satan. Now it means getting over negative feelings.

At one time, the freshly Christianized saw the horror of Satan's work within themselves; *they would have no more of it.* They realized the utter mercy of God that saved them and felt it was completely reasonable to live out their lives on the battlefield. Gratitude to God made the load light and the cost of war easy to accept.

Many of today's Christians find this concept repulsive. No wonder! They initially were drawn to the gospel by promises of emotional well-being and exemption from the pain of life.

Emotional well-being *is* a blessing from God; our error is that we have made it a great goal. According to God's Word, *seeking the Kingdom* is the goal and all these other things will be added.

"But seek ye first the kingdom of God, and his righteousness; and all these things shall be added unto you." (Matthew 6:33)

I have watched with dismay as entire congregations reduce the purpose of Christian living into *getting over past hurts.* If this becomes a life-long pursuit, we are in for disaster! We will never field an army or mount an attack. We will hand over an entire generation to the devil by default. Yes, we need to take the time for the wounded among us to be healed, but their recovery must be our intention and battle preparedness must be our goal.

How then do we live in the knowledge of war and become effective soldiers?

(1) *"Thou therefore endure hardness, as a good soldier of Jesus Christ."* (II Timothy 2:3)

If I believe I am in war, it provokes me to guard my life.

I will zealously remove any clutter or entanglement that jeopardizes my ability to hear and obey my Commander-in-Chief.

(2) *"Dearly beloved, I beseech you as strangers and pilgrims, abstain from fleshly lusts, which war against the soul."* (I Peter 2:11)

Temptation is an act of war against my soul.

Away with casual attitudes toward personal sin! I must forsake them immediately. Temptation is not a fly we swat away but a bullet we dodge.

(3) *"Finally, my brethren, be strong in the Lord, and in the power of his might. Put on the whole armour of God, that ye may be able to stand against the wiles of the devil. For we wrestle not against flesh and blood, but against principalities, against powers, against the rulers of the darkness of this world, against spiritual wickedness in high places."* (Ephesians 6:10–12)

I must put on all the armour.

I have no right to expect protection if I do not accept the reality of war. In war, armour is deadly serious business. If I have not given each piece of armour close attention, if I have not meticulously put it all on, then *I am vulnerable.*

The key word in all these verses is "all." All the armour must be on and I must do all to stand.

(4) *"He teacheth my hands to war, so that a bow of steel is broken by my arms."* (Psalm 18:34)

I will seek out training on how to fight. Turning from defensive Christianity to attack Christianity is not easy, if I have been consumed with surviving and merely gaining inner peace.

We must resolve to learn attack skills, to be educated on the rights and responsibilities of our war. We can be confident, however, because our trainer is the best there is and victory is inevitable for trained Christian soldiers.

(5) *"I therefore so run, not as uncertainly; so fight I, not as one that beateth the air: but I keep under my*

body, and bring it into subjection; lest that by any means, when I have preached to others, I myself should be a castaway." (I Corinthians 9:26,27)

"This charge I commit unto thee, son Timothy, according to the prophecies which went before on thee, that thou by them mightest war a good warfare. Holding faith, and a good conscience; which some having put away concerning faith have made shipwreck." (I Timothy 1:18,19)

"Hereafter I will not talk much with you: for the prince of this world cometh, and hath nothing in me." (John 14:30)

I must win the first war.

My first battlefield is me; flesh must be wrestled into submission. Paul referred to his own body, that it must be brought under. My eating habits, my rest schedule, my efforts to get adequate exercise, all reflect war. A massively obese Christian contradicts his message. Likewise, Paul warned Timothy to fight for a good conscience.

Before we enter the great war, this first battle must be won. I must go into the great war with bodily desires in check and a spirit that has conquered jealousy, pettiness, judgmentalism, and fear.

(6) *"For though we walk in the flesh, we do not war after the flesh (for the weapons of our warfare are not carnal, but mighty through God to the pulling down of strongholds)."* (II Corinthians 10:3,4)

I must find the weapons I have been gifted to use.

I must know that pulling down strongholds is my imminent goal. I can do it; I must do it; I'm gifted and trained to do it!

Each of us has a unique way of using God's weaponry. We must find our own weapon and learn its proper use.

(7) *"Proclaim ye this among the Gentiles; prepare for war, wake up the mighty men, let all the men of war draw near; let them come up; beat your plowshares into swords, and your pruninghooks into spears: let the weak say, I am strong."* (Joel 3:9,10)

I must join the great army. A true soldier never breaks rank. Meaningful attacks are waged by entire armies acting as a single being.

Linking hearts and gifts together with other believers is the key to victory.

Drop out of the social Christian scene and enlist in the army of God. Find those other warriors who, like you, have hearts ablaze to do what those heroes of faith did.

"Who through faith subdued kingdoms, wrought righteousness, obtained promises, stopped the mouths of lions, quenched the violence of fire, escaped the edge of the sword, out of weakness were made strong, waxed valiant in fight, turned to flight the armies of the aliens." (Hebrews 11:33,34)

Defeating Satan and glorifying God in battle are the greatest exploits a believer can have.

So get on with it!

IMPORTANT PEOPLE DO IMPORTANT THINGS

There is an unseen factor at work within us which does more to influence our lives than we ever imagine. To the poor or underprivileged, it is an invisible chain that traps them in the ghetto. To the successful it is a vulture that denies them any sense of accomplishment. The victims of this unseen force have very similar symptoms. They either cannot advance in the face of opportunity or they feel like failures even after they succeed.

The presence of this unseen force is detectable in many of God's people. They feel deprived and unworthy of God's best and never see themselves as participants in spiritual dynamics.

Important people do important things!

Look at that statement. What it means is that an inner sense of value produces a valuable life. True accomplishment is not sporadic. An important leader is not a flash in the pan. Why do some march through life confidently turning opportunities into lasting achievement while others are gripped by a new strain of self-destructive emotions? The culprit has been given various names: low self-esteem, inferiority, and dozens of other things.

Every year over 5,000 teenagers commit suicide because of this feeling. One out of four women in America has a food disorder serious enough to take her life. As many as 30 percent of all Americans live in a cloud of depression dangerous enough to require professional counselling. Experts are justifiably alarmed and have concluded that these inner feelings of worthlessness are the number-one enemy of modern Americans.

Even in the church most pastors agree that while conditions aren't as severe, the same epidemic is at work.

Satan hurt America deeply by disintegrating the family. Now we see the inevitable fallout of a society that has done just about everything to belittle parenthood and especially fatherhood. We have become a generation of emotionless orphans. We have realized almost too late that parents give children the self-worth that makes them successful adults.

"Train a child in the way he should go, and when he is old he will not turn from it." (Proverbs 22:6 NIV)

The centerpiece of our personality is the self-definition and direction that parents impart. Millions do not have that. Consequently, they are nomads in search of relief from an inner ache they don't even understand.

It is not surprising that one of the most widely read books today is one written by Scott Peck entitled THE ROAD LESS TRAVELED. In it the author echoes this very theme: "The feeling of being valuable—I am a valuable person—is essential to mental health and is a cornerstone of self-discipline. It is a product of parental love. Such a conviction must be gained in childhood; it is extremely difficult to acquire it during adulthood. Conversely, when children have learned through the love of their parents to feel valuable, it is almost impossible for the vicissitudes of adulthood to destroy their spirit."

What hope is there for this orphaned generation? What can Christians do to settle this storm within them? To the world it is a virtual impossibility but for the children of God there is a mighty solution. Certainly we need to restore our relationship with our parents if it is broken down. But that will not heal the void. We cannot undo a bad childhood but we can supersede it!

Thank God that Paul the Apostle faced a similarly vexed generation, a generation alienated from family by pagan chaos. God used him as a master builder of true children of God. What was his secret? He taught *adoption!*

Today we preach rebirth but we leave out adoption. What we get are people with an experience but still no father. Paul taught a formal transference of parenthood to God himself.

"For you did not receive a spirit that makes you a slave again to fear, but you received the Spirit of sonship. And by him we cry 'Abba, Father.' The Spirit himself testifies with our spirit that we are God's children." (Romans 8:15,16 NIV)

Hebrews 12:9,10 delves even deeper. *"Moreover, we have all had human fathers who disciplined us and we respected them for it. How much more should we sub-*

mit to the Father of our spirits and live! Our fathers disciplined us for a little while as they thought best; but God disciplines us for our good, that we may share in his holiness."

This means literally that the damage of childhood can be undone by a new father who acts on our personality for our good. What is the potential of such an experience? If parents can instill confidence in their children that helps them throughout their entire lives, what can God do if He is allowed to become a functioning father? He knows us completely. He can speak to our condemning heart and override it with love and confidence.

"No one who is born of God will continue to sin, because God's seed remains in him; he cannot go on sinning, because he has been born of God."
(I John 3:9 NIV)

He is mightier than any of our bad memories. Joshua is a textbook example. Gripped by a sense of total inadequacy and a slave childhood, he feared the future. Compounding his problem was the legend he had to replace: Moses.

Moses was the ultimate leader, trained in Pharaoh's palace, a military genius, an expert in leading people, with the added mystical dimension of the miracles that followed him. A confident man could not have replaced Moses, much less the son of a slave. Joshua needed much more than a formula for success. God had to pierce the deepest cavern of his spirit and flood it with the reality of God his Father. God thundered to Joshua, *"As I was with Moses, so I will be with you."*
(Joshua 1:5 NIV)

God gave Joshua his true identity, affirming him as a son equal to his predecessor, Moses. In the presence of his *true* father, Joshua's slave-child mentality was overcome. The son of a conqueror emerged. His voice now would ring with royal authority and great exploits would be the natural extension of his newfound identity.

Whereas Moses spoke to the Red Sea, Joshua would speak to the Jordan River. Whereas Moses commanded fire to fall from heaven, Joshua would command the sun to stand still in the sky. He would be remembered for the shout that brought down the walls of Jericho.

I wrote the first draft about Joshua while sitting in a cafè. When I got to the part about Jericho, the piano player across the room suddenly began playing "Joshua Fit the Battle of Jericho!"

If Satan can capitalize on our low self-esteem, he can convince us that moral awakening is not possible in our time, that it belongs to a better grade of believer. The end-time exploits we are destined for will be delayed if we see them as gifts for someone more deserving.

Your real Father is waiting for you. He longs to impart true self-worth. His gentle yet mighty voice will dispel a lifetime of hurt and disappointment. You may not emerge perfect from one session with your Father but a single dose of Fatherhood will make an amazing difference on how you see yourself and how you react to life. You will come back for more. You will start to notice opportunities that are rightfully yours that you previously overlooked.

If the number of confident Christians could multiply

and become the general consciousness of the Body of Christ, revival would be automatic.

In a world of emotional orphans, news of the true Father will create a rush to God unparalleled in history. But it all begins with you. Don't be like the brother of the prodigal son who never knew the goodness of his father even though he was at home. You'll never feel important until He says you are. Once He does, you will never settle for less than doing important things.

IT'S TIME TO REOPEN THE FORGE

Joseph could have thought God was strange because every time he received a message from God, he got into trouble. He dreamed that his brothers would bow down to him but he made the mistake of telling them, causing great trouble.

Some people are naive and think that a true message from God brings immediate blessing. Joseph found out that a dream from God can get you sold into slavery.

Joseph was no simple slave; in him was the root of greatness. God was honoring Joseph with a precious time of testing.

God had deliberately hidden His purpose so that this boy could become a man for the ages. Here was a vessel that would rise to high honor and save the nation of Israel from extinction. A weapon was being forged into divinely-controlled adversity.

Here was a test of Joseph's confidence in God's goodness. Can God be trusted? Does He know what He is doing? Can His children be secure in affliction and know they will come out strong? Can we reckon that our present trial is working something in us that is of eternal value?

Adversity; affliction; testing; trials. These words are not popular in our current world of escapism. The American pursuit of the carefree, painless life has influenced the church and, sadly, even the pulpit.

We look around and see gospels of temporal success and pleasure that go down easily and bring a pleasant tingle to the ear.

We must admit that this "good life" message entertains but I know that we secretly wonder why there are few spiritual giants today. Why don't we see an impact against demonic power in our cities?

Where are the men of steel who once shut the mouths of lions, exposed prophets of Baal, and pointed bony fingers at evil kings? Where are these champions who could preach chains off souls and ignite truth in the backslidden people of God?

Does our insistence on a life free of pain also produce a life devoid of power? Have we created a doctrine that makes no room for suffering or testing?

Escapism has stripped the church of power and we know it. We can't declare the power of God's grace to take us through because we don't want to go through, we want to go around.

We can't shout unto God with the voice of triumph because our comfortable distractions have reduced our battle cry to a petulant whimper.

The Philistines knew how to dominate God's army. They attacked and plundered the land but they especially saw to it that the forges were closed.

"Not a blacksmith could be found in the whole land of Israel, because the Philistines had said, 'Otherwise the Hebrews will make swords or spears."

(I Samuel 13:19 NIV)

Close the forges and you stop the weapons from being produced. Too many forges of faith are closed today. The weapons to shatter Satan aren't being produced.

Where are the blacksmiths of God today?

Are they ignored? Have they despaired because there is NO market for the gospel of greatness? Have they been trampled under the current "feel-good" shopping spree? Have they themselves been seduced by a lifestyle of ease and no longer want to provoke excellence in God's people?

Rarely do we hear the hammer of preachers pounding the white-hot steel of a fervent church into weapons that can change America. All too often all we hear is the tinny voice of the cookie cutter clones of comfort.

It's time to reopen the forge! That was the cry of God to the Laodicean church.

"You say, 'I am rich; I have acquired wealth and do not need a thing.' But you do not realize that you are wretched, pitiful, poor, blind, and naked."

(Revelation 3:17)

So what is the solution for the flabby Laodiceans?

Reopen the forge!

Abandon the drowsy life; break free of your drunken stupor! In verse 18 of Revelation 3, God the blacksmith says, *"I counsel you to buy from me gold refined in the fire so you can become rich."*

Satan desperately wants the forges closed; he fears the sound of fire refining saints; he cowers before the tempered steel; he flees from purified faith.

Deep within you there is a cry to walk in the might

of God. You long to be clothed in anointing that shatters chains of injustice. You want a guileless tongue that commands the powers of darkness to surrender.

What hinders us is our fear of the forge. Our flesh sees only the pain and it wrestles to stay alive. We must command ourselves! The forge is our friend because its temporary pain yields eternal benefits. We submit to the forge because we love God and we hate Satan. Today we suffer and are tried but tomorrow we will arise in His likeness!

Satan not only discredits the forge by passing off a painless, materialistic gospel but he also uses the opposite extreme.

There are those who dwell on the pain. They morbidly describe God's dealings in their own lives.

There are voices today that bitterly castigate the Christians for their lifestyle in America. *The fact is that God's mercy endures forever.* Wherever He finds a repentent heart, He will forgive, and He will make us mighty through Him to the tearing down of strongholds.

The forge is not something to fear nor is it a place to live. We should neither be afraid of it nor obsessed by it!

We must fact the fact that we have largely ignored the work of the blacksmith without then overemphasizing it.

To tolerate unnecessary suffering is unnatural; to avoid divine correction is unprofitable.

It takes discernment and maturity to make a distinction between an attack of Satan and a God-appointed time in the forge.

The same Jesus who with a word expelled hordes of demons was also driven by the Spirit into the wilderness to be tested. Paul said, *"He learned obedience by the things He suffered."* (Hebrews 5:8)

Right in front of you is an opportunity to apply this principle. *If a pestering satanic cloud hangs over you, it is your duty to resist it loud and long. If, however, you are under the blacksmith's care, you can obtain grace to triumph even in the furnace.*

Escapism can actually rob us in two ways:

First, because an escapist hates confrontation, he will tolerate Satan rather than resist. That person ends up living well beneath his rights and God-given privileges.

Next, the escapist avoids the furnace that will purify and fashion a true weapon. Either way, the "escape" mentality robs the believer of victorious living.

Joseph rose out of a dark cell to rule over Egypt. The forge had done its work. The years of suffering became a memory as they gave way to permanent victory. I can hear God whisper to Joseph while he was in the prison cell, "Just a little longer and you'll be ready to save a nation . . . take more of my grace."

Joseph didn't enjoy suffering; he respected it. He trusted the God who was behind all of it.

No greater words were ever spoken than those of Joseph to his brothers, *"You meant it for evil but God meant it for good!"* (Genesis 50:20)

Let's reopen the forge and learn the ways of triumph. The transformation from escapist to overcomer stings at first, but it leads to glorious results.

Right now Satan sneers and laughs but I have news

for him . . . the Blacksmith is fanning the forge. The same God who created Joseph, Daniel, and Elijah is rolling up His sleeves to make something out of us that will stun America and send Lucifer running in terror!

Stand before God and declare with all your heart, "I want to be forged; I want to glorify your Name as it has never been done before!"

For information on other books, tapes and video cassettes by Mario Murillo, please write or call:

MARIO MURILLO MINISTRIES
P.O. Box 5027
San Ramon, CA 94583

415-820-5470